D1250833

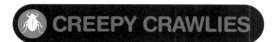

CREEPY CRAWLIES

The Life Cycle of
Fleas

NEW
FOREST
PRESS

An Hachette Company

First published in the United States by
New Forest Press, an imprint of Octopus Publishing Group Ltd

www.octopusbook.usa.com

Copyright © Octopus Publishing Group Ltd 2012

Published by arrangement with Black Rabbit Books
PO Box 784, Mankato, MN 56002

Library of Congress Cataloging-in-Publication Data

Twist, Clint.
The Life Cycle of Fleas / by Clint Twist.
p. cm. -- (Creepy Crawlies)
Includes index.
Summary: Describes the life of a flea by explaining its body parts, habitat, and behaviors. Explains how fleas carry diseases, passing sicknesses as they jump to new hosts. Includes life-cycle diagram and close-up photos of body parts--Provided by publisher.
ISBN 978-1-84898-520-9 (hardcover, library bound)
1. Fleas--Life cycles--Juvenile literature. I. Title.
QL599.5.T86 2013
595.77'5--dc23
2012003597

Printed and bound in the USA

16 15 14 13 12 1 2 3 4 5

Publisher: Tim Cook   Editor: Margaret Parrish   Designer: Steve West

Series Consultant: Dr. Richard Vane-Wright

Picture credits:
b=bottom; c=center; t=top; r=right; l=left
Alamy: 1, 8 (Papilio), 6, 9, 21t (PHOTOTAKE Inc), 6-7 (M I (Spike) Walker), 8-9 (Juniors Bildarchiv), 15t (imagestopshop), 23 (Jack Sullivan). Ardea: 21 side panel (Steve Hopkin). Bananastock: 16-17. Corbis: 12-13 (CDC/Phil). FLPA: 7 (Albert Mans/Foto Natura), 22b (Heidi & Hans-Juergen Koch/Minden Pictures). Getty Images: 17t (Image Makers). NHPA: 1, 14 (Stephen Dalton). OSF: 12. Science Photo Library: 9 side panel (CNRI), 10 (Volker Steger), 11t (Dr. P. Marazzi), 11b, 11 side panel, 18t, 18b, 19, 20b, 20-21 (K.H. Kjeldsen), 13 side panel (Martyn F. Chillmaid), 19 side panel (Peter Chadwick), 24 (Eye of Science), 25t, 25b (David Scharf), 26 (VVG).

Contents

What is a Flea? 4

Up Close and Personal 6

Hairy Homes.................................8

Blooduckers 10

Passing It On...............................12

Waiting for a New Home 14

Biggest Jumper...........................16

Scattered Eggs...........................18

Finding a Host 20

Fleas and Humans......................22

Bloodsucking Relatives................24

More Bloodsuckers......................26

Life Cycle and Fabulous Facts.............28

Glossary 30

Index 32

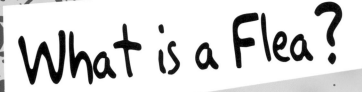

What is a Flea?

Fleas are small, wingless insects. They are so small they are hard to see. Fleas may be small, but they can jump amazing distances... and they bite!

Bats usually have lots of fleas, since fleas can spread easily when the bats are roosting.

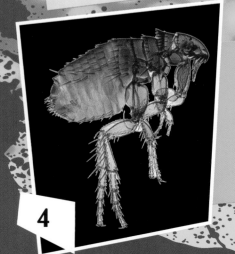

Fleas feed on blood, but they are not predators. Predators kill their prey before eating it, but fleas take blood from living victims. Creatures that live this way are called parasites.

These fleas live on a dog's nose.

Who's Who?

Insects belong to a group of animal known as arthropods. Adult arthropods have jointed legs but no inner skeleton. Instead, they have a tough outer exoskeleton. All insects have six legs when they are adults, and most have at least one pair of wings, although some have two pairs.

Fleas make their homes on the skins of mammals and birds. Animals that have parasites living on or in their bodies are called hosts.

Fleas have six legs and are insects.

Up Close and Personal

Fleas have the same body type as other adult insects: they have a head, thorax, and abdomen.

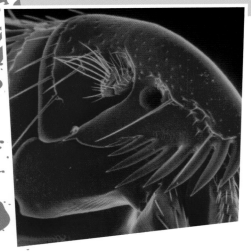

The head of a cat flea magnified 40 times

Abdomen

A flea's head contains antennae, a brain, and a mouth. Most fleas have eyes, although they have poor eyesight. Some do not have eyes.

The abdomen is the largest part of the flea's body and contains the digestive system.

The thorax is the middle part, where the legs are attached. The flea's back legs are stronger than its front and middle legs.

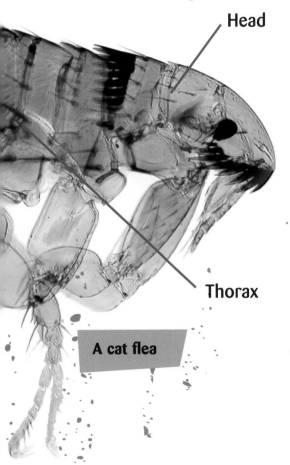

Head

Thorax

A cat flea

The body is narrow and flat and covered in bristles.

Six Legs

Insects are sometimes called hexapods because they have six legs ("hex" means six in Latin). All insects are hexapods, but not all hexapods are insects. Springtails, for instance, have six legs but are not true insects.

Don't let the leg count fool you. This springtail isn't an insect.

Hairy Homes

A flea uses its sharp claws to grip the soft skin of its host. Its narrow body lets it slip easily between the hairs or feathers that cover the host's skin.

Mammals groom and scratch their fur to try and get rid of parasites such as fleas. Birds preen their feathers for the same reason.

When a cat has fleas, it will scratch itself repeatedly because flea bites itch.

Cat fleas have backward pointing hairs to help them to stay on their scratching hosts.

When animals try to scratch fleas away, the spines and bristles catch on the host's hairs or feathers and prevent the insect from falling off.

On the Outside

Animal parasites can be divided into two groups: ectoparasites, which live on the outer surface of the host, and endoparasites, which live inside the host's body.

Tapeworms live in fleas, which are bitten off and swallowed by the host animal and settle in its digestive system.

Bloodsuckers

A flea's mouth is made for drinking blood. A pair of hollow, needlelike stylets pierce the host's skin so the flea can suck its blood.

When the flea drinks, its abdomen swells with blood. Fleas prefer to eat daily, but they can go months without feeding.

A cat flea's head is helmet-shaped to make it easier to move through the cat's fur.

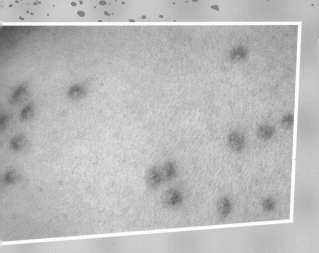

These nasty red marks are flea bites.

A flea bite is painless at first. After a few minutes, however, the host's skin reacts to substances on the flea's stylets—the bite begins to itch, and the host starts to scratch. But by this time, the flea has moved on.

Barbed Security

Stylets contain tiny upward-pointing barbs. If the flea is detected while it is drinking, the barbs dig into the host's flesh and make the flea difficult to shed. Some species of flea stay attached to their host's skin for days, holding on tightly with their barbs.

The bloodsucking stylet is in the center.

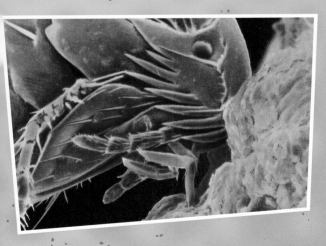

This cat flea is sucking its host's blood.

Passing It On

Unfortunately, a flea is much more than just an itchy nuisance. It can also spread deadly diseases.

A single bite does not cause much harm by itself. The real problem is the blood the flea carries with it.

This rabbit flea can spread myxomatosis.

When a flea sucks blood from one host and then moves to another, it brings some of the first host's blood with it.

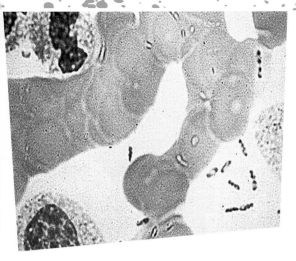

Magnified view of microbes in a drop of blood

Infected blood contains millions of disease-causing microbes. Blood in the flea's stylet transfers microbes to the second host, spreading disease.

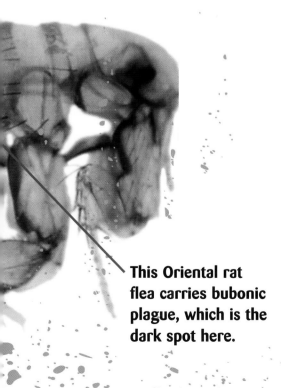

This Oriental rat flea carries bubonic plague, which is the dark spot here.

Rabbit Killer

Rabbits are pests because they eat crops. In Europe and Australia, rabbit fleas were used to kill rabbits. A few rabbits were infected with a disease called myxomatosis and then released. Fleas carried the disease from rabbit to rabbit, killing about 95 percent of the rabbit population in a few years.

This rabbit has red and swollen eyes, which is a sign that it has myxomatosis.

Waiting for a New Home

When a flea can't find a host, it can go for weeks or even months without feeding while it waits for the right host to come along.

When a host dies, its fleas are forced to move because they cannot eat blood from a dead animal. If the host lives in a crowded place, like a bat roost or rabbit warren, the fleas don't have to look far.

Fleas leap on to a new host to find a fresh supply of blood.

A pet cat can pass its fleas on to its owner.

If, however, the host lived alone, the fleas may have to wait a while before a new host comes along.

Fussy Fleas

Fleas are usually choosy about where they live. Most fleas like a particular host speicies. Rabbit fleas, for instance, live only on rabbits, and chicken fleas like chickens. Some fleas, however, are not so fussy. Cat fleas, for example, are happy to feed off other species, including humans.

Fleas like close living quarters.

Cat fleas are not finicky about the host they choose.

Biggest Jumper

A flea usually stays still or slowly moves over skin looking for a good spot to feed. When it needs to, however, a flea can move farther and faster than any other living creature.

When it has to make a quick getaway, a flea can jump about 200 times its own body length. This is the equivalent of a human jumping over a 40-floor skyscraper in one leap.

Fleas accelerate more than 20 times quicker than the fastest jet planes.

You'll never outjump a flea!

Stored Power

The secret to the flea's jumping ability is its back legs. Muscles in the back legs store energy in the same way that a stretched rubber band does. When the muscles are triggered, they release this stored energy in one powerful burst and propel the flea high into the air.

The power is in the back legs.

Scattered Eggs

Male and female fleas mate only if they have recently drunk fresh blood. After mating, the female continues to lay eggs for as long as she has a daily supply of blood.

Females spread their eggs all over the host's skin.

The droppings, egg (above), and larva (below) of a cat flea

The eggs hatch into tiny larvae that are unable to drink blood. The larvae get their taste for blood by eating the blood-rich droppings of the adults.

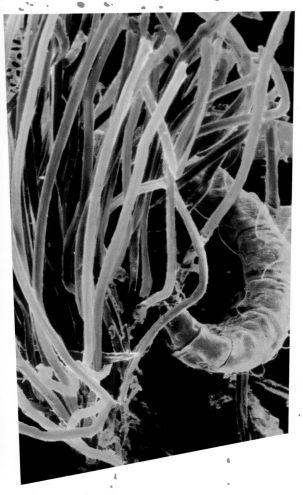

This cat flea larva cocoon is in a carpet. When a host comes by, the larva will hatch and jump on.

Within a month, the larvae are grown and they pupate. Flea larvae spin themselves cocoons made of a silklike substance. Inside the cocoons, the pupae have to wait for the right moment before emerging as adult fleas.

Development

Insects develop from eggs in two ways. With many insects, including fleas, the eggs hatch into larvae that look different from the adults. The larvae go through a stage called metamorphosis when they change into adults. With other kinds of insect, such as cockroaches and grasshoppers, the eggs hatch into nymphs that look like little adults.

A grasshopper nymph looks a lot like its parents.

Finding a Host

For fleas, pupation takes between six days and six months; after that, an adult emerges from the cocoon. The pupa waits until a suitable host is nearby. It then emerges and hops on board.

The pupa can't see, but it can tell when a host is close. It uses other senses for the task.

Two cat flea cocoons

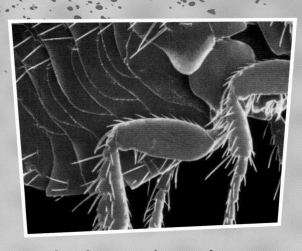

Tiny bristles sense heat and movement.

Leg bristles can detect the slightest movement. The vibrations a host makes when walking by let the pupa know it's time to hatch.

temperature Sensitive

Fleas are so sensitive to temperature they can find a host in complete darkness by sensing its body heat. Pupae have the same keen sense. Pupation ends as soon as the hungry flea senses its host, emerges, and leaps straight onto its meal. Adult life has begun.

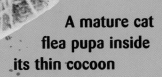

A mature cat flea pupa inside its thin cocoon

A cat flea nestled in cat fur

Fleas and Humans

It is not surprising that humans—the most widespread mammals on Earth—are host to their very own species of flea.

Human fleas are found wherever people live in dirty, crowded conditions. A few hundred years ago, fleas were an uncomfortable part of daily life—everyone, rich and poor, had fleas.

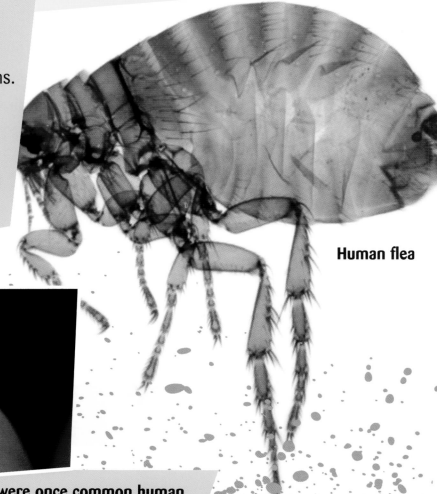

Human flea

Fleas were once common human pests; this one is being squashed.

Although human fleas are no longer common, headlice are. This girl is being treated for headlice.

A fleabite swells, itches, then disappears. The bite does no real harm, but it can result in the death of the host if the flea is carrying disease-causing microbes. Fleabites can spread dangerous diseases such as typhus and bubonic plague.

Black Death

In the 14th Century, the Black Death (bubonic plague) killed one-third of Europe's population. Rat fleas carried the microbes that cause bubonic plague, and in the filthy conditions of the time, the fleas spread the disease from rats to humans.

Victims of the Black Death are being carried away.

Bloodsucking Relatives

Fleas are a very uniform group of insect. For the most part, they look and act the same, although there are exceptions.

The pregnant chigoe flea burrows into the flesh of the host, usually in its feet. Once settled, she lays her eggs, which cause intense itching. A chigoe flea is sometimes called a "jigger," and this is where the confusion begins.

Chigger

Another relative, called a chigger, also burrows into its host's feet. But a chigger is not a flea, or even an insect. It is the larva of a type of mite. The larvae can bite through skin and bury themselves in the feet of animals, where they feed on their hosts' flesh. Chiggers itch even more than jiggers, and they both pass on diseases.

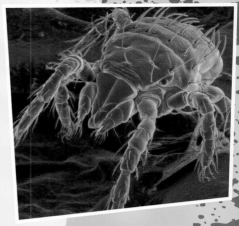

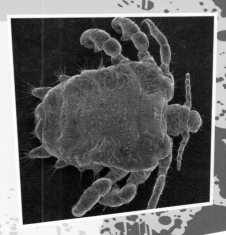

Lice

Lice are insects that like to live on the skin of animals. Some lice suck blood, but others do not. Bird lice, for example, feed on fragments of feathers. A few lice do a bird no harm, but having too many can cause the bird to lose its feathers.

Crab louse

The crab louse is a bloodsucker that lives in human body hair. They have strong claws for gripping onto hairs, and females produce special glue to stick their eggs in place. Both young and adult crab lice feed on human blood, but they are not known to carry diseases.

More Bloodsuckers

Fleas are not the only creatures that live by drinking blood.

Mites

Mites are tiny arachnids and are related to spiders and ticks. Some feed on plants, but others are parasites on animals. The varroa mite is a problem for beekeepers because the mite lays eggs inside honey bee colonies. When the young mites hatch, they feed on the bee larvae.

Ticks

Ticks are small arachnids, usually less than ½ in (1 cm) long, that live in much the same way as fleas. All ticks are parasites that attach themselves firmly to a host to suck blood. Some ticks cause painful illnesses such as Lyme disease.

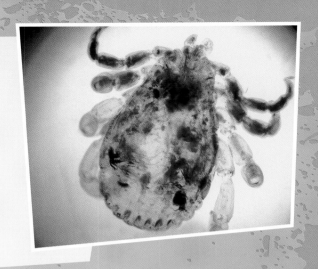

Mosquitos

Mosquitos are small flying insects that must feed on warm blood to breed. Mosquitoes have a very different lifestyle from fleas. They lay their eggs in water, and the larvae hatch as water animals, developing wings during pupation. Mosquitoes can carry deadly diseases like malaria and yellow fever.

Leeches

Leeches are related to earthworms, but they live very different lives. Earthworms burrow in soil and eat dead plants. Leeches spend lots of time in water and feed on blood from fish, amphibians, and other animals. Leeches were once widely used in medicine to remove blood from patients. They are sometimes still used this way.

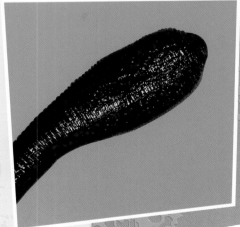

Find Out More

Life Cycle

A flea egg is white and tiny (about 0.5 mm). When the egg hatches (after 1 to 10 days), the larva emerges and feeds on adult droppings. After 5 to 11 days, the larva spins a cocoon and becomes a pupa. The pupa stays in the cocoon until it senses a host nearby. It then emerges from the cocoon, leaps onto the host, and begins feasting.

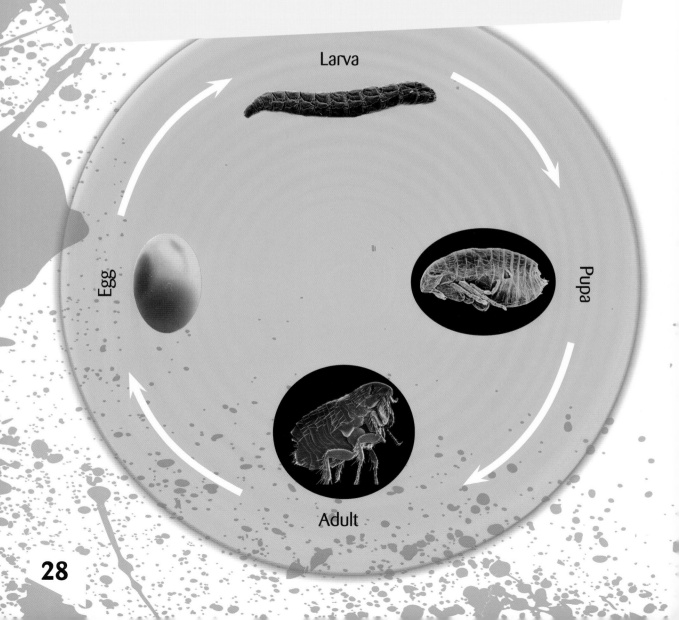

Larva

Egg

Pupa

Adult

Fabulous Facts

Fact 1: Fleas have been around for 100 million years.

Fact 2: Fleas can jump around 200 times their own length.

Fact 3: Cats and dogs can wear collars or be treated with flea-killing poison to get rid of fleas.

Fact 4: A female flea lays about 2,000 eggs during her life.

Fact 5: The female flea consumes 15 times her own body weight in blood daily.

Fact 6: The flea's life cycle can be completed in as little as 16 days.

Fact 7: The most common flea is the cat flea.

Fact 8: Once a pet gets fleas, its surroundings must be completely cleaned or the pet will be reinfested.

Fact 9: A dog flea can live and breed on a dog for more than 100 days.

Fact 10: There are over 2,000 species of flea.

Fact 11: Flea eggs are smooth and often fall off the host into surrounding carpets and bedding.

Fact 12: In the past, everyone had fleas. People are cleaner now, so today it is not as common for humans to have fleas.

Fact 13: If a flea falls from its host, its tough exoskeleton will prevent it from being killed on impact.

Glossary

Abdomen—the largest part of an insect's three-part body; the abdomen contains many important organs.

Acceleration—an increase in speed.

Antennae—a pair of special sense organs found at the front of the head on most insects.

Arachnid—a group of animal, with four pairs of legs and a two-part body, such as spiders, mites, and ticks.

Arthropod—any creepy crawly that has jointed legs; insects and spiders are arthropods.

Barb—a sharp point facing the opposite direction on a weapon or tool that prevents it from being taken out of the victim.

Black Death—an outbreak of bubonic plague that killed about one-third of Europe's population in the 14th century.

Bubonic plague—a disease that normally affects wild rodents, but which can be passed to humans by flea bites.

Cocoon—a protective covering of silk produced by some insect larvae to protect their bodies while they transform into adults.

Digestive system—the organs that are used to process food.

Ectoparasite—a parasite that lives on the outside of a host's body.

Endoparasite—a parasite that lives inside a host's body.

Exoskeleton—a hard outer covering that protects and supports the bodies of some creepy crawlies.

Host—an animal that can provide food and a home for parasites.

Insect—a kind of creepy crawly that has six legs; most also have wings.

Larva—a wormlike creature that is the juvenile (young) stage in the life cycle of many insects.

Lice—a group of small insect parasites often found on birds and mammals; some lice suck blood, some feed on dead skin.

Mammal—a group of warm-blooded animals that have an internal skeleton and that feed their young on milk.

Microbes—tiny living things, so small that they can only been seen through a powerful microscope.

Myxomatosis—a disease of rabbits that is caused by microbes carried by rabbit fleas.

Nymph—the juvenile (young) stage in the life cycle of insects that do not produce larvae.

Parasite—any living thing that lives or feeds on or in the body of another living thing.

Pupa—an insect larva that is in the process of turning into an adult.

Pupation—the process by which insect larvae change their body shape into the adult form.

Rodents—a group of small mammals that includes rats and mice, but not rabbits or shrews.

Roost—a resting or sleeping place used by birds and bats.

Skeleton—an internal structure of bones that supports the bodies of large animals such as mammals, reptiles, and fish.

Springtail—a six-legged creature that is not, in fact, an insect because it does not share the same DNA as other insects.

Stylets—the hollow, pointed parts of a flea's mouth that are used to pierce skin and suck blood.

Thorax—the middle part of an insect's body where the legs are attached.

Typhus—a killer disease that can be passed to humans through flea bites.

Vibration—a quivering motion.

Index

A
abdomen 6–7, 10, 30
acceleration 17, 30
adults 5, 19, 21, 28
antennae 6, 30
arachnids 26–27, 30
arthropods 5, 30

B
barbs 11, 30
bats 4–5, 14–15
bees 26
beetles 7
birds 5, 8–9, 25
bites 11, 23
Black Death 23, 30
blood
    diseases 12–13
    food 4, 10–11
    larvae 18
bloodsucking insects
    10–11, 24–27
bristles 7, 9, 21
bubonic plague 23, 30

C
cat fleas 5–9, 29
    cocoons 20–21
    head 10–11
    larvae 18–19
    mouthparts 11
    hosts 14–15
chiggers 25
chigoe fleas 24
cleanliness 29
cockroaches 19
cocoons 19–21, 28, 30
crab lice 25

D
digestive system 30
    fleas 7
    tapeworms 9
diseases 12–13, 23,
    27, 30
dogs 5, 29
droppings 18–19

E
earthworms 27
ectoparasites 9, 30
eggs 18–19, 28, 29
endoparasites 9, 30
energy storage 17
exoskeleton 5, 29, 30
eyes 6

F
feet bloodsuckers 24–25
female fleas 18, 24, 29
food 4, 10–11

G
grasshoppers 19

H
head 6–7, 10–11
headlice 23
hexapods 7
honey bees 26
horses 5
hosts 5, 8–9, 30
    blood 10–11
    detecting 20–21
    diseases 12–13
    humans 22–23
    larvae 18–19
    waiting period 14–15
humans 22–23
    bites 11, 23
    cat fleas 15
    cleanliness 29
    crab louse 25
    jumping power 16–17

I
insects
    bloodsuckers 10–11,
    24–27
    development 19
    legs 7
    parasites 9
    understanding 5, 30

J
jiggers 24

jumping power 16–17,
    29

L
larvae 30
    chiggers 25
    fleas 18–19, 28
leeches 27
legs
    bristles 21
    insects 5, 7
    muscles 17
lice 23, 25, 30
life cycle 28–29

M
mammals
    diseases 12–13, 23
    hosts 4–5, 8–9,
    14–15, 22–23, 30
    humans 11, 15–17,
22–23, 25, 29
    see also cat fleas
mating 18
microbes 13, 23, 30
mites 25, 26
mosquitoes 27
mouthparts 11
muscle power 17
myxomatosis 12–13, 31

N
nymphs 19, 31

P
parasites 4–5, 9, 24–27,
    30–31
pets see cat fleas; dogs
plague 13, 23, 30
predators 4
pupae 19–21, 28, 31
pupation 19–20, 21, 31

R
rabbit fleas 12–15
rat fleas 13, 23
rodents 5, 13, 23, 31
roosts 14–15, 31

S
senses 20–21
skeleton 5, 29, 31
spines 7, 9
springtails 7, 31
storing energy 17
stylets 10–13, 31

T
tapeworms 9
temperature 21
thorax 6–7, 31
ticks 27
typhus 23, 31

V
varroa mite 26
vibrations 21, 31

W
wings 5